500

ALL TIME FUNNIEST JOKES & STORIES ABOUT SEX

Sheila & Ron Stewart

500
ALL TIME FUNNIEST
JOKES & STORIES
ABOUT SEX

ISBN: 0-9717617-0-1

Published by

Acadia Scale Press

For Bob & Maureen

500

ALL TIME FUNNIEST JOKES & STORIES ABOUT SEX

"What part of a man determines whether he needs sex or not?"

"The part he's married to."

Wife: "I have a headache."
Husband: "Would an aspirin help?"
Wife: "No. But flowers would be nice."

During romance, a woman feels ecstasy from the tip of her nose to the tips of her toes.

With men it's a little more centralized.

A husband who had been in the dog house for several days was complaining to another husband.

"My wife doesn't even bother saying no when I ask if we can fool around," he said. "That would be too much like admitting she was talking to me."

"Since your wife became pregnant, does she ever make requests regarding sex?"

"Yes. Just last night."

"What did she say?"

"Please, not while I'm throwing up."

First wife: "My husband came into our bedroom last night and made love to me for an hour and a half."

Second wife: "My husband can do that. It might take him a few more trips, but my husband can do that . . . ."

Boyfriend: "What will it take to persuade you to make love to me? Flowers? Jewelry? Expensive dinners? Weekends at a resort? A world cruise?"

Girlfriend: "O.K."

Wine can heighten the sexual experience. The trick is to have enough to heighten the experience, but not so much that you fall asleep or throw up.

A couple had been married for twenty-five years. The wife wanted more in their love making than just sex.

"You could bring me flowers and take me out for dinner once in a while," she said.

"I already did that," he answered.

"Our wedding day doesn't count," she replied.

"How do you tell when your wife is really angry with you?"

When she says, "Not tonight . . . Sir."

A husband had been reading one of his wife's romance novels.

"How did you enjoy it?" a visitor asked.

"Much too long," the husband replied. "Eight hundred pages. It once took the author twenty pages just to write a love scene. I could have done that in two lines."

He wife interrupted, "Sometimes less . . . ."

Husband: "Want to fool around?"

Wife: "Flowers would be nice, first."

Husband: "They only last three days, and then they die."

Wife: "That reminds me. The garbage needs to be taken out."

Husband: "What about fooling around?"

Wife: "Sure. Why not. After you take out the garbage."

Wives were discussing romance.

"Has your husband ever brought you flowers?" one asked.

"No," another replied, "but he once bought me some gardening equipment."

"I've decided to stop wasting my life on stupid, idiotic, trivial, stressful, absolutely nothing to be gained nonsense that doesn't lead anywhere."

"You're giving up men again, aren't you."

"My wife found a long blond hair on my collar."

"Is she curious about where you got it?"

"Even I'm curious about where I got it."

4

Two husbands are talking.

One says to the other, "I asked my wife if she was in the mood. She said, yes. But I think I'm going to have to be more specific."

"Why is that?"

"She went shopping."

"Is your husband a good lover?" one wife asked another.

"He's a terrible lover," answered the other wife. "But at least he's better than your husband."

"Oops . . . ."

First husband: "I'm angry at my wife because we're not getting as much satisfaction from our love making as we should."
Second husband: "Why are you blaming your wife?"
First husband: "Who else would I blame?"

First husband: "My wife says I'm a really lousy lover. Has your wife ever said that to you?"
Second husband: "I can't say that I've ever heard her mention your name."

As my wife grew older, she didn't look quite as desirable as she used to, until a friend told me what he was paying his young wife in alimony. My wife began to look *real* desirable.

"My wife and I finally found the time to talk about the incompatibilities in our marriage and the problems we're having with sex," one husband informed another.

"That's nice," the other husband answered. "When?"

"Just this morning," the first husband replied, "room three, down at the courthouse."

"The first thing a man should do when he asks a woman to go to bed with him is proclaim his honesty and pure intentions."

"What is the second thing?"

"Try to get her name."

A husband thought he would beat his wife to the punch. He said, "Do you have a headache tonight?"

She answered, "No, that's tomorrow night. Tonight I just don't feel like it."

Children were discussing the birds and the bees in school.

"This is pretty tame stuff," one of them said, "compared to what my parents say they have to go through."

Going all the way: For a woman, sex. For a man, emptying the bank account in hopes of getting sex.

"I expect my wife to be an equal partner in our sexual relationship," one husband said to another. "And if she isn't, I let her know about it."

"Really?" the other husband replied. "What do you say to her?"

"WAKE UP!!!!"

Two children were talking.

One asks, "How long did it take your mother to make you?"

The other replies, "She told me nine months of hard labor. How long did it take your mother to make you?"

"She told me, one night of extreme pleasure."

"I think I like your mother's way better."

A wife described her evening as two hours of romance and then mad passionate love with her husband.

"Your husband must be quite the lover," another wife said.

"Oh no," she replied. "He was only there for the last few minutes. The rest of the time I was watching a love story on T.V."

In the old days we had sex. Now there are more ways to have sex than the number of times we had sex.

"My wife just informed me that she married me for my wonderful physique," one husband said to another. "Excuse me, but I have to go out and shovel snow."

A husband and wife were having an argument. The husband thought he had won when he said, "Not only that, making love to you isn't all that great either."

His wife responded, "If you think it isn't all that great now, wait until you've been without it for a month."

A wife goes to her doctor. She wants to have children. The doctor says for her and her husband to make love for a month and then come back and see him.

A month later, the wife returns. "How did you and your husband make out?" the doctor asks.

"Not too good," the wife replies. "He quit after twenty-three hours."

They call women the fair sex: "Have you seen the way they use sex ... ???!!!"

First wife: "Before you were married, your husband said he would make love to you every minute, every hour, of every day. How is he doing?"

Second wife: "He got the minute part right."

"My wife is trying something new to enhance her sexual pleasure," a husband said.

"Really?" another husband replied. "What is it?"

"Caffeinated coffee."

"What does that do?"

"It keeps her awake."

A husband telephones his wife.

Husband: "I've planned an exciting evening out for us. Dinner for two at your favorite restaurant, front row seats for that new play you've been wanting to see, an evening of romance, and then mad passionate love."

Wife: "Who is this . . . ?"

A man went into a house of ill repute and asked the madam how much it would cost to have sex.

"Two hundred and fifty dollars," she informed him.

Thirty seconds after he began, he was finished.

As he left, he said to the madam, "You sure don't get a lot for two hundred and fifty dollars."

A husband wanted to introduce fantasy role playing into their sexual relationship, but his wife didn't completely understand the concept.

He suggested that she pretend to be a lonely housewife looking for companionship, and that he would pretend to be a handsome meter man who makes a pass at her.

In the middle of their love making, she said, "The other meter man doesn't ask me to do this."

"I found a new way to entice my husband into the bedroom," one wife said to another.

"Does it work all the time?" the other wife asked.

"Yes," the first wife replied, "except when I'm too tired."

"To have sex?"

"To carry the T.V. into the bedroom."

Husband: "Am I still the greatest lover in the whole wide world?"

Wife: "No."

Husband: "But last night you told me I was the greatest lover in the whole wide world."

Wife: "Last night I wanted sex."

"I told my husband that I enjoyed sex, but I also wanted some foreplay," a wife said.

"And did he agree to it?" she was asked.

"Yes," she replied. "But he said he would like to have the sex first."

Temptation: Something that men and women run away from, or run toward, depending on the mood they're in.

"What can a woman do if she wants to delay the completion of the sex act?" one wife said to another.

"Just whisper some words in his ear," answered the other wife.

"Such as?"

"Such as, is that my husband I hear coming up the stairs . . . ?"

A husband and wife agreed that each time they made love, the wife would put money away so they could use it on their vacation.

After a while her husband asked, "How are we doing?"

She said, "Not bad, I've already bought the tickets."

He asked, "Where are we going?"

She said, "Which movie would you like to see."

A husband informed his wife that it had been so long since they made love, he couldn't even remember.

"It was two days ago," she said.

"No it wasn't," he replied. "It was almost two weeks ago."

"Ah ha," she exclaimed. "You do remember."

The difference between great sex and not so great sex: About an hour . . . and two minutes.

Two wives were discussing birth control.
"I'm trying out a new type of pill," one said.
"What is it?" asked the other.
"A sleeping pill."
"How is that supposed to work?"
"I give it to my husband."

A husband was lining up the T.V. antennae for better reception. He asked his wife to let him know when there was a clear picture.
"Is it there yet?" he asked.
"Yes," she replied.
"What?" he asked again.
"Yes," she yelled back.
"What?"
"YES."
"What?"
"YES!"
"What?"
"YES . . . !! YEEESSS!!! YEEESSSSS!!!!"
The next morning their next door neighbor stopped them on the street and said, "Boy, you two must have had a good time last night."

"My husband moves really fast in the morning. For instance, he gets up at 7:30 and by 8:00 he's at work."

"What happens if you feel like making love before he goes to work?"

"O.K. 8:02."

"My wife and I agreed that we would each pay the other what we felt it was worth every time we had sex, and after a year we would pool our resources."

"How much did it come to?"

"Three thousand, one hundred and two dollars, and fourteen cents."

"Where did the two dollars and fourteen cents come from?"

"That was my wife's share."

"Doing anything interesting this evening?" one wife asked another.

"Nothing too exciting," the other wife answered. "Other than, I just told my husband that we could have sex."

"Did that make him happy?"

"I think so. Right now he's jumping up and down on the bed."

Two women were enjoying a refreshment in a bar.

"Men don't have any manners," the first woman said. "How would you like to have one come up to you and say, O.K. Honey, just let me know right now, are you prepared to put out tonight, or what?"

"A man said that to you in a bar?" the other woman exclaimed.

"No," the first woman answered. "My husband said that to me last night in our bedroom."

"I haven't made love to my wife in more than a week."

"Why not?"

"Would you make love to someone who falls asleep in the middle of sex?"

"No."

"Well, neither will my wife."

Romance is simple. A woman sends out signals. All a man has to do is figure out what signal she's sending, who she's sending the signal to, and if the signal she's sending is really what she has in mind.

Social intercourse: A form of casual conversation a man strikes up with a woman. Often the only intercourse he'll be getting.

"My wife doesn't understand sex," a young man who was recently married said to a friend. "We were making love, and I was explaining what a climax was, and she kept saying, not so fast."

A patient went to his doctor.

"I can't sleep," he said.

"Have you tried sex?" the doctor asked. "Sex can sometimes act like a medication that will relax you enough to let you get to sleep."

A week and a half later, the patient returned.

"It took seven days," he said, "but it worked."

"I wonder why it took seven days?" the doctor answered.

The patient replied, "It took me six days just to find the medication."

Women do not make fools of men.

Men do that on their own.

Women just help.

"So I said to my wife, a man's home is his castle, and when he demands sex he expects to get sex."

"And what did your wife say?"

"I'm not quite sure. Sound doesn't carry too well to the spare bedroom."

Women are so unappreciative. You give them thirty seconds of the best sex they ever had, and they don't even say, thank you.

A husband divorced his wife because their sex life was not satisfying.

Upon receiving the first alimony check, she informed him, "I don't know about you, but I certainly feel more satisfied."

"I gave my husband a photograph of himself for our anniversary," one wife said to another, "and he gave me a house and half a million dollars."

"That must have been some photograph," the other wife exclaimed.

"Yes," the first wife replied. "He turned out very well. His girlfriend was a little fuzzy . . . ."

A young woman says to her fiancé, "After we're married, I'll make love to you for breakfast, for lunch, for dinner, anytime you want."

Her fiancé answers, "That's all well and good, but who's going to make my meals?"

"Did you tell George that two minutes is more than enough time for a woman to have a climax?" George's second wife asked his first wife.

"No," the first wife said. "Why do you ask?"

"Oh, no reason," the second wife replied. "I'm just trying to figure out where he got the idea."

A man who was not having much success with women was praying to his guardian angel.

"I pray," he said, "that tonight and every night until I die, my bed will be filled with the sexiest, most gorgeous women in the world."

"Granted," said the guardian angel. "The first of many sexy, gorgeous women will be arriving at your bedside tonight at nine o'clock."

"Great," the man said. "Out of curiosity, just how many more years do I have until I die?"

"You're due to go at four o'clock this afternoon."

"I once had a May-October romance with an older man," one young woman said to another.

"Don't you mean May-December romance?" the other young woman asked.

"No," the first young woman replied. "I mean May-October romance. That's when his wife caught us."

A husband was trying to simplify his description of the sex act.

"Sex is extremely easy," he said. "It's just a matter of not trying to put a round peg into a square . . . ."

His wife interrupted. "Just where are you learning this stuff?"

"My husband made love to me for three minutes last night."

"Three minutes . . . ?"

"Yes. Three minutes. He usually takes only two minutes."

"Two minutes . . . ? And last night he made love to you for three minutes . . . ?"

"Yes."

"Why the difference?"

"Last night I insisted on foreplay."

Two husbands were talking.

"I suggested to my wife that we should put some fantasy into our love making," said one.

"And what did she say?" asked the other.

"She said it was O.K. with her," the first replied. "She said that I could be a tall dark stranger, and she would be a mysterious virgin."

"And how was it?"

"I don't know. I haven't found her yet."

"I'm a little concerned that my wife might be losing interest in sex. I told her that while she was out shopping today, to pick up a month's supply of contraceptives. She brought home a three pack."

A girlfriend was having to fight off demands from her boyfriend to have sex.

She said, "I'm saving it for a rainy day."

He said, "It's raining now."

She said, "Not enough."

"Have you ever paid for sex?" a husband was asked.

"Not until after I got married," he replied.

First husband: "That's the last time I try that approach."

Second husband: "What approach?"

First husband: "My wife and I hadn't made love for a while, so I thought I would approach it gradually."

Second husband: "And . . . ?"

First husband: "I said I would like to do something we hadn't done for a while."

Second husband: "So, what happened . . . ?"

First husband: "We got the garden weeded and the car washed . . . ."

"My wife gave up sex for Lent."
"What's wrong with that?"
"It's her seventh Lent this year."

And then there was the little boy who said to his mother, "Boy, oh boy, oh boy, oh boy, I can hardly wait to grow up and have sex, the way my big brother has sex."

"Did you see your brother having sex with a woman?" his mother exclaimed.

"No," the little boy replied. "I saw him in the bathroom. But what's this thing about a woman?"

"When we were young, my wife and I would talk for two hours, make love for two hours, then talk for another two hours," a husband said.

"What do you do now?" he was asked.

"Pretty much the same," he replied, "except for the middle part."

Newlyweds were given a book as a wedding gift titled 'Five Hundred Ways To Make Love'. A few days after they returned from their honeymoon they were met by the friend who had given them the gift.

"Well, how did you make out with the book?" the friend asked.

"Really well," the husband said. "We finished it by the end of the first week."

The friend's mouth dropped open.

"Don't feel bad," the husband replied. "We had three other books."

A friend met a newlywed bride a few weeks after the wedding.

"Have you ever had sex twice in one day?" she asked.

"No," the happy bride replied. "We're just not ready to cut back that far yet."

Some men were doing a little bragging about their sexual accomplishments and how many times they could perform in one night. Finally, they turned to an elderly gentleman.

"Let me see," he said. "First there was 1:30, then there was 3:15, then 6:10, 8:20, 10:05, and finally 12:15."

"Wow!" one of the younger men exclaimed. "How did you manage to do that?"

The elderly man furrowed his brow and looked at the other men. "Does he always get this excited when someone makes love six times in twelve months?"

"My husband bought me a book about sex."
"Do you use it?"
"I sure do. I hit him with it when I'm not in the mood."

First wife: "My husband promised me last night that I would feel ecstasy of a magnitude that I will never feel again."
Second wife: "And will you be looking forward to feeling it again?"
First wife: "I don't know. I'm not really sure what I'll be looking for."

"Do you still spend the same amount of time making love as you did when you were young?" an old timer was asked.

"Sure do," he replied. "Two minutes."

"How do you ever manage to finish sex in two minutes?"

"I stop and catch my breath a lot."

"I read that wives sometimes use sex to get even with their husbands," one husband said to another.

"My wife would never do that," the other husband replied. "She just stops giving it to me."

A husband's memory was slipping, so his wife helped him out.

"I can't remember the last time we made love," he said

"It was just last week," she answered.

"How many times did we do it?" he asked.

"Five," she replied.

"Did we enjoy it?"

"We had a great time."

"How about making love tonight?"

"I gave it to you five times last week. You want it again already . . . ?"

24

First woman: "Have you ever been seduced?"
Second woman: "Yes. Just this afternoon."
First woman: "How was it?"
Second woman: "Not bad. The cake was O.K., but the icing was a little rich."

Young children were looking at an expectant mother's pregnant tummy.

"I asked my parents what causes this," one of them said. "Nobody seems to know."

A mother decided to tell her daughter the truth about where babies came from.

"It's better than the story you told me about the birds and the bees," her daughter replied. "But I still prefer the one about the stork."

"Do men believe in sex before marriage?"
"Only if it's available."

Women sometimes fake orgasms. Men are lucky. They don't have to fake anything . . . at least until they begin talking to their friends about it.

"Is your older sister still a virgin?" one little boy asked another.

"I'm not sure," the other little boy replied, "but I've been watching her and her boy friend, and if she is, it's not by much."

A wife agreed to pretend she was an airline flight attendant so that her husband could pretend he was a passenger trying to seduce her. Now if he wants sex, she makes him check in two hours early.

"It sure will be nice to finally be married so I can have sex anytime I feel like it," a young man said to the other men at his bachelor party. "Why is everybody laughing . . . ?"

Two husbands met in Hawaii.
First husband: "I asked my wife to name the most exotic place on earth that she would like to make love. She said Hawaii. So I made reservations."
Second husband: "And how has it been?"
First husband: "I wouldn't know. I haven't seen her since we got here."

My wife is very considerate. How many wives do you know who would make up the sofa for you.

A husband scoffed when his wife suggested he try to be more romantic like the leading man they were watching on television.

"For an hour and a half he doesn't even know he's in love with her," he said, "then when he does decide he's in love with her, it only takes him ten minutes to chase her, talk her into it, have foreplay, make love, and then fade out until morning. I've been doing that for twenty years."

Wives were discussing children. One was asked if she would like a baby that looked like her husband.

"No," she replied. "I would like a baby that looks like the tennis pro that lives down the street, but the neighbors might talk."

"Last night my wife and I made love. I never heard such screaming."

"Your wife screams . . . ?"

"No. The neighbors downstairs."

"I think my girlfriend could be warming up to possibly having sex with me," a young man confided to a friend. "She said that if I treat her to a romantic dinner, bring her flowers, buy her an engagement ring, and marry her . . . maybe someday."

"My wife has been saying, not tonight, a lot lately, so I gave her a book on French lovemaking."
"What does she say now?"
"Not tonight, Cheri."

"Have you ever fantasized about making love to a woman you can't have?" a man was asked.
"All the time," he replied.
"What does your wife have to say about your fantasies?" he was asked.
"Not tonight. I'm too tired."

When it comes to bargaining power, women withhold sexual favors.

Men also bargain by withholding sexual favors. They just aren't able to withhold the favors quite as long.

Two hours of sex to a man: Includes an hour and fifty-eight minutes of talking her into it, and thirty seconds of foreplay.

Husband: "I'm not in the mood for sex."
Wife: "Tonight, you married the right person."

"Man has been making love since the beginning of time."
"Boy, he must be tired."

Drive In Theater: Where young people go to enjoy a bad movie.

Incurable romantic: Best cure that has been found so far - a good dose of alimony payments.

Boyfriend: "Did you enjoy our foreplay."
Girlfriend: "Is that what we were doing?"

Erection: What a woman does for a man's ego when she goes, "Ohhhh, ahhhh, eeeeeeeeeee!"

Wife: "There must be something that could put some more spice into sex."
Husband: "I'm game."
Wife: "I wasn't talking to you."

First husband: "Your wife makes friends very easily."
Second husband: "Thank you. Now get out of our bed."

Men were discussing lack of sex.

"They say that abstinence is good for the mind," said one.

"I'm surprised I'm not more intelligent," replied the other.

A husband made a deal with his wife. He would take her to Las Vegas three or four times a year, and she would provide him with sex.

After they were married for thirty years, he began to suspect that she was getting the better of the deal. It's not that they weren't both getting what they wanted. It was just that she appeared to be getting what she wanted more often.

A wife demanded, "I want flowers, I want jewelry, I want romance, I want an expensive dinner, I want an hour of foreplay, and then maybe we'll make love."

"What about ordering a pizza?" her husband suggested.

"All that will do is put you to sleep," she said.

"I know" he replied.

A wife said, "I have a headache."

Her husband answered, "Don't worry about it. That's not the part I'll be needing."

A man had been asking a woman to go out with him.

"For the millionth time, no," she exclaimed.

"What? Are you giving up already?"

"Does it take you and your husband longer to complete the sex act now that you're getting older?" one retired woman asked another.

"Slightly," the second retired woman replied. "The last time, it took us three and a half hours."

"To finish . . . ????!!!"

"To get started."

My wife got a book on planned parenthood from a feminist group. It was all right with me, until I discovered I wasn't part of the plan.

"I'm concerned about my daughter," one mother said to another.

"Why?" the other mother asked.

"She says she might be pregnant," the first mother said.

"Do you know who the father is?"

"Yes. That wealthy businessman on the next street. Fortunately, he says he'll marry her and give her everything she will ever need."

"Then why are you concerned?"

"I'm concerned she's not pregnant."

A husband and wife are watching a handsome actor in a romantic movie.

"Why can't you make love to me like he does?" the wife asked.

"If you pay me what they're paying him, I'll give it a shot," the husband replied.

"Do you come from good breeding?"

"My father says it was very enjoyable."

"I'm not too sure about my wife's new method of birth control."

"Why? What does she do?"

"Before we begin, she says to me, well, do you feel lucky?"

"My wife is a fortune teller. She even knows which nights sex will be enjoyable and which nights sex will not be enjoyable."

"That's amazing. How does she do it?"

"I don't know. I just know that every few days I hear her say, you will not be enjoying sex tonight."

A man goes into a bar with a woman. She is wearing a brand new dress and expensive jewelry, she has recently manicured nails, a fresh hairdo, she looks like a million dollars.

"It's getting more and more expensive to persuade a woman to go to bed with you," he complained to another man at the bar. "All these new clothes, the jewelry, the price of hairdos and make up, I'm telling you, the cost is killing me."

"Why don't you just marry her," the other man suggested, "and avoid all those costs?"

"I did marry her," the first man replied.

Two women are talking.
One asks, "Have you lost your virginity?"
The other answers, "Yes. Several times."

"Is your new bride a versatile lover?" one husband asked another.

"I'll say!" the other husband answered. "She has already come up with thirty-two ways to say no."

Woman in bar: "I'm flattered that you would ask me to spend the night with you, but I can't, I'm married."
Man in bar: "How about tomorrow night?"

An elderly man went to his doctor.

"Something is wrong," he said. "My wife and I made love all right the first time, but I had difficulty getting an erection the second time."

"That's perfectly normal," the doctor assured him. "It sometimes occurs when you try to have sex twice in one night."

"What one night," the elderly man replied. "That was last year."

A woman goes into a jewelry store and asks for something sexy and provocative.

The jeweler looks puzzled. "Something sexy and provocative . . . in jewelry . . . ?"

"Yes," she replies. "My boyfriend gave me his charge card and told me that when we make love tonight he'd like me to wear something sexy and provocative."

Wives were discussing golf. One of the wives left the room to get refreshments. By the time she returned, the conversation had turned to sex.

"Is your husband better now than he used to be?" she was asked.

"Not really," she replied. "But I think his accuracy could be improving."

Ecstasy: For a man, sex, any sex. For a woman, sleep, any sleep.

"My wife and I still have sex regular as clockwork," one elderly man said to another, "and always at exactly the same time."
"Every day!!!????"
"Fourth of the month."

35

"Do you believe you have better luck getting younger women to go to bed with you, or getting older women to go to bed with you?" one man asked another.

"I believe I have better luck getting younger women to go to bed with me," the other man answered.

"I wonder why that would be?" the first man said.

"I'm not sure," the other man replied. "I just know that I have better luck when I believe a woman is twenty-five than when I believe she is forty-five."

"In the heat of passion, has your wife ever called you by another man's name?"

"Yes. Lots of times."

"Really? When?"

"Anytime she watches a romantic movie on television. Sometimes I'm Cary Grant, sometimes I'm Clark Gable, sometimes I'm . . . ."

"My date told me he expected something in return for all the money he spent to buy me dinner," one woman said to another. "For seven dollars, I let him hold my hand for two minutes."

"Where is your husband today?"

"In the hospital."

"What happened to him?"

"A ménage à trois."

"What's a ménage à trois?"

"It's when a man makes love to two women at the same time. He said he had always wondered what it would be like."

"So why is he in the hospital?"

"Because I hit him five times with a frying pan."

"You hit your husband five times with a frying pan because he was wondering what a ménage à trois would be like . . . ?"

"No. I hit him five time with the frying pan because that's how many times it took before he saw two of me."

Some married men were providing inspiration to a newlywed husband.

"Just tell her that husbands expect sex anytime they ask for it, and that's that," one of the men informed him.

The newlywed looked across the room where wives had formed their own group with the new bride. After a moment, he replied, "You tell her."

Husband: "It says in this magazine that there are four hundred and fifty-eight ways to make love."

Wife: "Well, only four hundred and fifty-seven more to go."

"My husband said that I was going to have to put more excitement into our sex life," one wife informed another.

"And did you?" the other wife asked.

"Yes," the first wife answered. "My new husband is very exciting."

Why is it? The way to a man's heart is through his stomach. The way to a woman's heart is through a jewelry store.

Why is it? No matter which man a woman decides to marry, her mother thinks she should have married the other one.

Why is it? When children are bad, they take after the father's side of the family. When they are good, they take after the mother's side.

Parents were attempting to explain sex to a young child. After they finished their descriptions of the male and female bodies, the youngster said, "It sounds O.K., but what's the connection?"

One husband's explanation for completing their love making in two minutes was because he heard somewhere that too much sex was not good for a person.

A husband informed his wife, "I was thinking about experimenting with some new and erotic ways to make love."

"Let me know how you make out," his wife replied. "I'll be in the other room."

"My husband and I like to turn the radio on when we're making love," one wife informed another. "When we were young it was rock music, fast and explosive. Then as we grew older it changed to waltzes, slow and rhythmic."

"What is it now?" the other wife asked.

"We're back to rock music."

"Fast and explosive?"

"No. Slow and rhythmic . . . if we're lucky."

"I think my husband could be finding sex a little more strenuous than he used to," one retired woman confided to another. "During our love making last night, he said, there must be an easier way to do this."

After a fight, a wife was asked if she and her husband were making love again yet.

"Right now," she said, "we're not even making eye contact."

"My wife and I have a rocky marriage. We have already separated three times and then got back together."

"Wow! How long have you been married?"

"Since three o'clock this afternoon."

"I'm not too sure about that woman I just tried to pick up," one man said to another in a bar.

"Why?" the other man asked. "What did she say?"

"She said to come back next Tuesday," the first man replied, "and she would try to fit me in."

Oversexed: A husband who asks for sex three or more times a night. For some wives, three or more times a week, or a month, or a year . . . .

If I wanted your opinion, I'd ask for it: What a penis says to a brain just before a man does something stupid.

Sex: A three letter word for people who have difficulty remembering four letter words.

A really good lay: Sleeping in on a cold morning.

Seconds: The amount of time it takes a man to romance a woman, have foreplay, make love, and fall asleep.

Sexual expressions: What a man goes through until he finds an expression that persuades a woman to say yes.

Variations: Making out in the kitchen.

Curious friends were talking to a young bride who had returned from her honeymoon.

"Did you experiment with different ways to make love?" she was asked.

"Yes," she replied.

"How many ways?" she was asked.

"Quite a few," she replied.

"What kind of ways, besides the normal position?" she was asked.

The young wife thought about it for a moment and then replied, "Just what is the normal position?"

"I'm sorry, I can't talk right now," one wife said to another who had telephoned. "My husband has been complaining that I haven't been giving him enough sex, and he made me feel so bad that now I'm on a guilt trip."

"Oh?" the second wife said. "Are you on the way to the bedroom?"

"No," the first wife replied. "I'm on the way to the mall."

Wife: "Not tonight. I'm tired."
Husband: "Don't worry. I won't keep you up long."

Two slightly intoxicated men met in a bar.

"The thing I missed most after divorcing my wife was the sex," one of them said.

"I know what you mean," the other man replied. "I'm having a similar problem myself."

"Oh, that's too bad," sympathized the first man. "Separated? Divorced? How many years?"

"Not talking," answered the other man. "Three days."

Two men met on the street. One of the men was carrying a bottle of wine.

"Where are you off to?" the other man asked.

"To my new girlfriend's house," the man with the wine answered. "I've heard the best way to seduce a woman is with wine."

An hour later, they met again.

"Where are you off to now?" the other man asked.

"For more wine," the first man replied.

Two wives were comparing husbands.

One wife says, "Each time we make love, my husband has a cigarette afterwards, and I worry that so many could cause health problems."

The other wife answers, "Not in our house."

"Would you say that your husband is a good lover?" one wife asked another.

"Some days he's a good lover, and some days he's not quite so good," the other wife replied.

"When is he good?" the first wife asked.

"When I'm in the mood."

First wife: "Do you think that husbands should expect sex any time they feel like it?"

Second wife: "Of course. Now ask me if they should expect to *get* sex any time they feel like it."

First wife: "Is your husband a good lover?"

Second wife: "He can be very entertaining."

"I think my wife might be getting over our little disagreement. Last night she told me, when hell freezes over. Tonight she told me, when hell freezes over . . . maybe a little sooner."

Women don't always say *no* when men ask for sex. Usually they can let us know *very clearly* without uttering a word.

Two men were watching a third man as he sat down to write a book.

"What's he going to write about?" asked one of the men.

"His sexual experiences," answered the other man.

"So what's he waiting for?" asked the first man.

"Experiences."

A son asked his father if he knew the best way to handle a woman.

"Tenderly and lovingly," his father replied. After a moment of thought he added, "And with just a slight amount of trepidation."

Man: "If you make love to me, I'll buy you dinner to make up for it."
Woman: "I don't think I could eat that much."

"I had a sexual experience with one of the models in that magazine," a high school student said, "but my mother brought an end to it."

"What did she do?" another student asked.

"She took away my magazine."

Some ten year old boys were trying to impress each other with how knowledgeable they were about sex. All except one.

"Heck," he said, "for the first three years of my life, I didn't even know what sex was."

"My sexual energy now just isn't the way I remember it being when I was younger," one husband said to another.

His wife interrupted, "His sexual energy when he was younger wasn't even the way he remembers it being when he was younger."

"Even love must have a beginning and an end," a husband said to his wife after sex that lasted only a few minutes.

"Yes," she replied, "but not at the same time."

A middle aged man was having a sexual fling.

"I'm going through my second childhood," he said.

"Is it any different this time than the first time?" his girlfriend asked.

"Yes," he replied. "I couldn't do this the first time."

"Last night my husband said to prepare myself for three and a half hours of ecstasy," one wife said to another.

"Did you have sex?" the other wife asked.

"Yes," the first wife answered.

"How was it?" the second wife asked.

"I was a little disappointed," the first wife replied.

"Three and a half hours of sex?" the second wife exclaimed. And you were disappointed? How could you be disappointed?"

"I thought we were going to the mall."

"I'm looking for some sexy lingerie," a wife said to a sales clerk.

"Are they for you?" the clerk inquired.

"No," she replied. "They're for my husband. I'll just be wearing them."

A wife took her husband to the hospital with a bump on his head.

"How did this happen?" she was asked.

"Sex," she answered.

"Too rough?" a doctor asked.

"No," she answered. "When I said yes, he fainted."

Wives were having a few laughs at the expense of their husbands.

"My husband has managed to delay his climaxes by fifty percent," one said. "That extra thirty seconds really means a lot to me."

Why women are called the opposite sex:

When a man is in the mood, they're not in the mood. When a man is not in the mood, they're in the mood.

Fortunately for men, they can get into the mood *real fast.*

"Sex is cheap. All I have to do is give my wife some flowers."

"How is that cheap?"

"Before we were married, it cost me flowers, dinner, jewelry, and a movie."

"So, how is your love life?" one man asked another as they surveyed the meager pickings in a bar.

"Steady," the other man replied.

"Getting a lot?"

"Not getting any."

Quickie: How a boyfriend goes out the window when a husband arrives home early.

Candy is dandy, but liquor is quicker: A good rule to remember, whether you want to have sex, or whether you don't want to have sex.

Casual sex: One way to explain why we haven't had any in six months.

Trying something different: Having the wife come to your side of the bed.

That special time of the month: When a husband says, "How about it," and his wife says, "Yes."

Sex on the side: If you don't know what you're doing, just say so.

Making love: Two people who don't know what they're doing, somehow managing to have a great time doing it.

First husband: "My wife has a sore back."
Second husband: "Has it affected your sex life?"
First husband: "No."
Second husband: "Aren't you afraid it might aggravate her back?"
First husband: "No. She doesn't move all that much."

"Do you want the $100.00 service or the $500.00 service?" a madam asked a potential customer.

"What's the difference?" he inquired.

"For $500.00," she replied, "you get to have sex before you climax."

"Would you like a glass of wine before we make love?" a man asked his new girlfriend.

"No," she answered, "but I might enjoy a diamond necklace."

A husband and wife were making love when the gas stove developed a leak and blew them clear through the roof of the house. On the way down the wife exclaimed, "I don't know what you did, but could you do it again."

Men were discussing marriage.

"I used to be happily married," one said.

"Oh, I'm sorry," another sympathized. "Are you separated, divorced, widowed ... ?"

"No," the first answered. "Still married."

Wives were listening to their husbands boast about their sexual stamina.

"I know how to shorten their stories to about two minutes," one of the wives said.

"How?" another asked.

"Tell them to explain it exactly as it occurred."

A husband and wife agreed to make love. The husband said for his wife to go to bed and that he would be along in a few minutes. When he arrived she was tossing and turning in an effort to get comfortable.

After watching for several seconds, he asked, "Have I missed much?"

"I can't believe the amount of nauseating, obscene, repulsive, vulgar smut I receive in Emails. Yesterday I was sent so many pages of pornography I could hardly read them all."

51

Husband: "I'm afraid I have some bad news. I was run over by a florist truck on the way home."
Wife: "So, did you bring me flowers?"

"My boyfriend left me when I informed him I wasn't quite ready to have sex with him," one woman confided to another.
"And you said he never did anything nice for you . . . ."

"Your wife appears to think the problem with your marriage is sex," a marriage counselor said to a husband.
"And I thought it was because we *weren't* having sex," the husband replied.

A husband was happy to learn he had won a contest to be on the first ten year space voyage around the solar system . . . until he discovered his wife had sent in his name five thousand times.

Wife: "I'm going to go to sleep now."
Husband: "I'm sorry. Are you still awake . . . ?"

"I think my wife and I might enjoy trying out that new contraceptive over there on the third shelf," a husband said to a clerk in the drug store.

"It's O.K. with me," the clerk replied, "but do you think you can get up there?"

"I once went out with a woman who told me she didn't go all the way," one man said to another.

"And what did you say?" the other man asked.

"I said to her . . . what *do* you do?"

"And what did she say?"

"She said, just about anything, except I don't go all the way."

"And then what?"

"I discovered you can have a lot of fun not going all the way."

Two elderly gentlemen were discussing love making.

"Are you grateful when you can still have sex?" asked one.

"I'm grateful when it doesn't kill me," answered the other.

"I'm really embarrassed. I went to the doctor because I was having difficulty getting an erection. He gave me a thorough examination and a prescription to be taken at bedtime."

"What's wrong with that?"

"He said that half a pill should do it."

"I would like to have sex with you," a young woman said to her boyfriend. "All I ask for is a little jewelry in return."

"What kind of jewelry did you have in mind?" he asked.

"A wedding ring," she replied.

Husband: "Will you love me forever?"
Wife: "Of course."
Husband: "Will you make love to me forever?"
Wife: "Don't push it."

Second husband: "I had sex with your ex-wife last night."
First husband: "How was it?"
Second husband: "She said I was worst man she ever made love to."
First husband: "Ha! I knew I wasn't the worst!"

Have you ever wondered if the snake in Adam and Eve stories was really a snake. If you ask me, he sounds more like a lecherous next door neighbor with a good line.

"Try it, you'll like it," he probably said.

I'll bet he was just named Snake.

"I think my husband might be cheating on me," one wife said to another. "We filled out one of those survey forms that asked how many times we make love. I said four or five times a month, he said three times a night."

"I've heard that the pleasure you derive from golf is a lot like making love," a non golfer said to a golfer. "Is that true?"

"I would say so," the golfer replied.

"In what way?" the non golfer wanted to know.

"Well," the golfer responded, "even when you're not very good at it, you can still have a lot of fun."

"What would you say is the most difficult aspect of golf and making love that would be similar?" the non golfer asked.

The golfer thought it over for a moment and then replied, "Probably getting a tee time."

I'm not sure I can afford my wife. I asked her what her idea of foreplay was. She suggested a European vacation.

Two children were talking.

"Sex isn't all that important to a man," said one.

"Who told you that?" asked the other.

"My uncle and my brother."

"How old are your uncle and your brother?"

"One hundred and six, and three and a half."

"I've forgotten more about love making than all these young men you see on T.V. will ever know," a husband of several years bragged.

"I've noticed," his wife replied.

"My wife is interested in trying a new sexual experience," a husband said.

"What kind of sexual experience?" another husband asked.

"I'm not quite sure what all is involved," the first husband replied. "I just know that when I asked if she'd like to try some erotic sexual positions she said, kiss my ass."

"My girlfriend and I had a really great relationship," one man said to another, "but she kept telling me there was something missing."

"Did you ever find out what it was?" the other man asked.

"Yes," the first man answered. "Just the other night, right when we were in the middle of making love."

"What?"

"Her husband."

"Last night when we were making love, my wife had a faraway look in her eye."

"Do you think it was ecstasy?"

"No. I think it was the exercise instructor down at her health club."

A wife refused to give her husband sex. Instead, she carried on a daily love affair with their chauffeur. Eventually, she divorced her husband and married the chauffeur. A few months after the wedding, the ex-husband ran into the chauffeur.

"How's married life treating you?" he asked.

"Not bad," the chauffeur replied, "but I sure do miss the sex."

"You know that sexy black negligee you were admiring in the lingerie store," a wife said to her husband. "I thought I would buy it and wear it for you on our anniversary."

After looking around for a calendar, her husband asked, "When is our anniversary?"

"A year from yesterday," she replied.

"Last night I asked my wife if she would rather have sex or read a book. She said that she would rather read a book."

"Did that upset you?"

"No. She was doing what she enjoyed, and I was doing what I enjoyed."

"What were you doing?"

"I was having sex."

A man and woman struck up a conversation in a nightclub, after which they shared a night of passionate love making.

"I'm usually not this free with my body," the woman said in the morning.

"You mean you don't usually have sex with men you meet in nightclubs?" the man asked.

"No," the woman replied. "I mean I usually charge two hundred dollars."

"How do you persuade your wife to make love when she's not in the mood?" a newlywed husband asked an older man.

"I just tell her a man needs it and that it's a wife's duty," the older man replied. "Occasionally I have to remind her how long its been . . . what's it been now . . . twelve years. Sometimes I'm forced to resort to more drastic measures . . . romance . . . dinner for two . . . flowers . . . ."

A newlywed husband liked to give his wife flowers and a romantic dinner before they made love.

"This is what we did on our wedding night," his wife told a friend, "and for some reason he still enjoys doing it."

"Why don't you tell him he doesn't have to do that anymore?" the friend said.

"Are you crazy."

"I predict a great loss in your life," a fortune teller said to a husband. "I see someone running off with your wife. No, no, wait, it could be your golf clubs they're running off with."

"Which is it?" the husband replied. "I need to make a tee time for the morning."

A wife delayed her shopping trip to the mall to have sex with her husband.

"Thank you," he said.

"That's O.K.," she assured him. "Most of the good stuff is gone in the first couple of minutes anyway."

"You should think of a woman's body as an oven," a wife said, "and sex as baking a cake."

"Just how does that work?" her husband asked.

"First you have to warm it up . . . ."

"If you were to compare all the very worst lovers in the world," one wife said to another, "I'm sure my husband would be one of the more romantic ones."

"What type of birth control do you and your husband use?" a wife was asked.

"Abstinence," she answered.

"How do you determine when to abstain?" she was asked.

"If we don't feel like it, we abstain," she said, "and if we do feel like it, we don't abstain."

"There's no winning with my wife. The last time we had sex I accused her of lack of interest. She accused me of shoddy workmanship."

In a sex education class, a college student was asked if he knew the most important step in putting a woman in the mood to make love.

After some thought he replied, "Coming up with the cash for drinks . . . ????"

"Is sex good for a person?"

"I'll say. I knew a man who made love three times every day until the day he died."

"How old was he when he died?"

"Fifty."

"What's so good about that?"

"He looked thirty."

A patient was suffering from fatigue.

Doctor: "It might be best if you reduce your physical activity for a while, including sex. Do you think you could do that?"

Patient: "I think I could do that."

Doctor: "How often do you have sex now?"

Patient: "I don't have sex now."

Nooner: Sexual relations at lunch hour when a man has thirty seconds to spare.

Childbirth: Something a husband says won't hurt. **Vasectomy:** Something a wife says won't hurt.

Obscene: To a man, dirty reading material he calls literature. To a woman, chocolate cake with a rich creamy filling.

Motel: A place where men go with their girlfriends. A place where women go with their boyfriends. A place where husbands and wives go to get away from the kids.

Sexual fling: What a man receives when a woman is not in the mood.

Chastity belt: "Ginger ale only please."

Why don't you come up and see me sometime?: A few kind words never hurt any penis.

"Is your husband getting used to your idea that sex is not an important part of marriage?" one woman asked another.

"He appears to be," the other woman replied.

"Did he tell you?" the first woman asked.

"No," the second woman answered. "I heard it from his new wife."

"Are they teaching you about the birds and the bees in school?" a young student was asked by his parents.

"We haven't gotten to them yet," the student replied. "We're still working on sex."

A frugal man went into the local drug store.

"That contraceptive you sold me has a hole in it," he said.

"Are you sure it has a hole in it?" the druggist asked.

"It must," the frugal man replied. "How else can you explain four children in five years?"

A husband said to his wife, "You know, men have been known to die because of lack of sex."

She replied, "Don't worry. I'll remarry."

"My girlfriend would never expect payment in exchange for sex," one man said to another. "She might accept small gifts, like jewelry, lingerie, dinners, plays, weekends at a resort, but payment, never."

Husbands were exaggerating how long they could make love.

"I sometimes enjoy making love for two hours," one bragged.

"Pfft," another answered. "After two hours of making love, I'm just getting ready to take my first coffee break."

"My husband sometimes finishes our love making in five minutes," one wife said to another.

"My husband is usually not that slow," replied the other wife.

A girlfriend insisted on expensive jewelry each time they had sex. Her boyfriend asked why they couldn't, every once in a while, just make do without all that. She said she didn't want to cheapen their love.

Woman: "I hate all men."

Man: "Does that mean you won't go out with me?"

Woman: "Are you asking me to go out with you?"

Man: "Yes, I am."

Woman: "I suppose I could make one exception."

Two elderly men were talking.

"I enjoy Chinese food," one said, "except I have it, and then I want to have it again."

"I'm the same way with sex," the other elderly man replied.

"Every day?" the first exclaimed.

"No," the second answered. "We only have Chinese food twice a year."

"My wife sure is gullible," one husband said to another. "I asked what she needed to put her in the mood to make love, and she said all she wanted was a bouquet of flowers."

"How does that make her gullible?" the other husband asked.

"I was prepared to go as high as a vacuum cleaner and an ironing board."

"A friend of mine was seriously injured during sex."

"What kind of sex was that??!!"

"The kind you have with your girlfriend when her husband walks in."

"Does making love make you sleepy?"

"Yes, but I'm usually able to finish."

"The trouble with sex," one retired man said to another, "is by the time you know everything, you can't do everything."

"Women are a lot more free with sex now," a college student said to an older man. "I'll bet when you were my age, you couldn't even make it to first base."

"True," the older man replied. "But I sure had a lot of fun trying to get there."

After a husband and wife had a fight, he asked if they could have make up sex.

She told him, "Why not." Actually, she told him several reasons why not.

"How many times have you and your wife made love?" a husband was asked on his first anniversary.

"Three," he answered.

"Only three? In a year?" he was asked.

"Yes," the young husband answered. "The other four thousand times were just sex."

A husband rented an adult rated video to put some spice into their love making. His wife made him take it back. There was no story.

A boyfriend left in a hurry when he heard a voice from upstairs, "Will you throw him out or will I . . .?"

A few minutes after he left, the cat was put out.

Two women at a nudist colony were comparing men.

"How did your date with your new boyfriend go last night?" asked one.

"Not very well," answered the other. "All he did all evening was try to get me to put my clothes on."

"Think of flowers, or a romantic dinner, or foreplay in the same way you would think about putting fuel in your car," a wife said to her husband.

"How is that?" he asked.

"Without them, you're not going anywhere," she replied.

Men have a tough time making decisions.

For instance, if a man had to choose between having sex or watching sports on T.V., he would have to think very hard before making a decision.

A woman, on the other hand, would have no difficulty at all making a decision between having sex or watching sports on T.V.

She'd go shopping.

"Before she would agree to marry me," a newlywed husband said to some other husbands, "my fiancée made me promise that I wouldn't demand sex more than once a day."

"Did that make it difficult for you?" he was asked.

"Not too difficult," he replied. "Up until then, I was hoping to get it once or twice a week."

"I was arrested last night, just because a policeman caught my girlfriend and me having sex in my car," one college student said to another.

"In Lovers Lane?" the other student asked.

"On Interstate 10," the first student replied.

A husband went to the doctor with a severely damaged penis.

"What happened?" the doctor asked.

"I went out drinking," he said, "and when I came home I wanted to make love to my wife."

"And I suppose she didn't want to," the doctor said.

"No, it wasn't that," the husband replied. "She was quite willing. The problem was me. I kept seeing three of her."

"So what does that have to do with your damaged penis?"

"I hit the floor three times, and the dresser twice."

Why is it?

If a book has five hundred pages, it won't sell. If a book has five hundred pages and one page of sex, it will sell like the dickens.

Two men were discussing shoe sizes. After mentioning that the size of feet could be an indication of the size of other parts of the male anatomy, one of them asked, "What size are your shoes?"

"I normally wear a size fifteen," the second man replied, "but I don't like to brag, so right now I'm wearing a size nine."

An elderly man with arthritis was heard complaining, "Everything is stiff, except the thing I want to be stiff."

"I can't seem to get women interested in me," one man said to another.

"Why don't you do what I did," said the other man. "I lost weight, I exercised, I dressed better, I looked after my appearance, and women began throwing themselves at me."

The first man decided to give it a try. A few months later when they met again, he said, "I don't understand it, I did everything you told me to do, but women still ignore me. What else did you do before they began to show interest?"

"Nothing, really," the second man said, "other than winning the five million dollar lottery."

"I might not be quite as good at this love making thing as I thought I was. While we were having sex last night, I suggested to my wife that we get a book on the subject to enhance our pleasure. My wife said it was a great idea and offered to look for one."

"What's wrong with that?"

"She offered to go out right then and look for one."

"What does your husband like to do when he's not bothering you for sex?" one wife asked another.

"Let's see . . . ," the other wife replied. "This morning, he had half a cup of coffee. What does your husband like to do?"

The first wife frowned. "He built a house, two garages, and a barn with sixteen stalls."

Men tend to have more difficulty displaying emotions than women.

Wife: "It wouldn't hurt if you showed a little romantic interest once in a while, such as flowers, or taking me out for dinner, or jewelry, or foreplay, or you could just say you loved me . . . ."

Husband: "A flower, you say . . . ."

I don't think it was a good idea to give my wife that book on modern love making. All I keep hearing is, "You can do what, and what, and what . . . and how, and how, and how . . . and where, and where, and where . . . ?" And then she keeps saying, "Why, why, why . . . ?"

One wife described their sex life as, "Some nights it's for the passion, some nights it's for the love, and some nights it's so my husband will let me go to sleep."

Why is it?
In the movies when a woman says she's going to slip into something a little more comfortable, she comes back in a negligee. At home, she comes back in her pajamas.

First divorced man: "I could always tell when my wife was in the mood to make love."
Second divorced man: "How?"
First divorced man: "She put on her sexiest clothes."
Second divorced man: "Then what?"
First divorced man: "Then she went to town."

"I asked my girlfriend if I could paint her in the nude."

"What did she say?"

"Yes."

"How did it turn out?"

"I didn't get it finished."

"Why not?"

"Every time she took off her clothes, I wasn't in the mood for painting anymore."

A man had sex with his girlfriend, in which he brought her to an exciting climax and left her so satisfied she fell asleep in exhaustion.

He knows this to be true, because when he asked if she had an exciting climax and was satisfied, she answered, "Oh yeah, sure, right. I'm real satisfied. I'm exhausted. Leave me alone. Let me sleep."

A husband was throwing some blankets and a pillow on the sofa in the living room when a friend dropped by.

With a greeting they often used when they met each other, the friend said, "Getting much?"

The husband growled, "Does it look like I'm getting much?"

"On a scale of one to ten, what would you give your husband in sex?" one wife asked another.

"I usually give him a two," the other wife said, "but there was that one time I gave him a seven."

"That's pretty good," the first wife said. "Was he particularly amorous that night?"

"No," the second wife replied. "That's how many minutes he lasted."

I don't think my wife is totally committed to the feminist movement.

She attended a protest gathering and burned her bra. Afterwards, she asked me if she could borrow ten dollars.

I said, "What for?"

She replied, "I need a new bra."

"My husband told me the sex we had in the middle of the night last night was the best sex we ever had," a wife said.

"How did you feel about it?" another wife asked.

"I was a little disappointed," she said.

"Why was that?" the other wife asked.

"I couldn't recall him waking me up to have sex," she replied.

Our neighbors have discovered a new way to have a satisfying sex life. She has sex with the delivery man, and he has sex with the lady down the street.

A wife was asked, "Have you ever cheated on your husband?"

"Is pretending to have an orgasm when you're not having an orgasm, considered cheating?" she asked.

Men were trying to impress each other by embellishing their sexual vitality.

"I don't know why they lie so much," one of their wives commented. "The truth would be much funnier."

A husband took refuge at a friend's house after his wife locked him out because he forgot their anniversary and his promise to take her out for dinner.

"I hope you're feeling really bad about what you've done," his friend exclaimed.

"I do, I do, I really do," the husband replied. "So what's for dinner?"

After making love to a school teacher, a boyfriend asked, "How was it?"

She said, "I'd give you a C."

He replied, "It sure felt like an A to me."

Women are better gamblers than men.

A boyfriend said, "I'll bet we have sex tonight."

His girlfriend replied, "I'll bet we don't."

She hasn't lost yet.

A man went to a psychic and asked, "Will I be having sex tonight?"

The psychic replied, "I have good news, and I have bad news. The good news is, you will definitely be having sex tonight. The bad news is, you will be having it by yourself."

A husband and wife gave their bed to guests during a visit, while they slept on the sofa. During the night they could hear the bed squeaking.

"Is the squeaking keeping you awake?" the wife asked.

"No," the husband replied. "But it is giving me an idea . . . ."

A man went to a doctor because he didn't seem to have any sexual energy.

"That's what happens when you try to burn the candle at both ends," the doctor informed him.

"Are you kidding," the man replied. "I'd be happy if I could just get my candle lit at one end."

As they snuggled into bed for the night, a husband and wife reminisced about the many years they had been happily married.

The wife asked, "In all those years, have you ever had difficulty remembering our anniversary?"

The husband answered, "Don't worry, I would never forget one of our anniversaries."

The wife replied, "O.K., which one was today?"

A couple went to a photographer. To lighten the mood, instead of asking them to say *cheese* when he was ready to take the picture, he told them to say *sex*.

The pictures didn't turn out quite as he expected. Every time he asked them to say *sex*, the husband repeated it with a big smile, and the wife said, "Not tonight, I'm too tired."

Man in bar: "I would go to the ends of the earth to have sex with you."
Woman in bar: "Go to the ends of the earth first. Then we'll talk about sex."

"We have friends who decided to join the mile high club," one husband said to another. "But I don't think they quite understand the concept."

"Why?" the other husband asked. "Where are they? Somewhere on an airplane?"

"No," the first husband replied. "They're somewhere on a peak in the Rocky Mountains."

"During our last airplane flight, my husband and I decided to join the mile high club," one wife said to another.

"How did you do?" the other wife asked.

"I'm afraid we didn't do very well," the first wife replied.

"How come?"

"We didn't have time."

"Why not?"

"Someone knocked on the door."

"So you didn't have time to have sex?"

"We didn't even have time to get our pajamas on."

"I once surprised my wife while she was preparing dinner," one husband said to another, "and I learned something about sex."

"What did you learn?" the other husband asked.

"I learned you should never attempt to get it while your wife is slicing vegetables."

"After a lot of drinking, I can live without sex for a while," one husband said to another.

"What made you decide that?" the other husband asked.

"Oh, I didn't decide it," the first husband replied. "My wife did."

"My wife said she was going to stop giving me sex unless I began bringing her gifts," a husband said.

"What did you bring her?" another husband asked. "Flowers?"

"No," the first husband replied. "Power tools."

"Power tools!" the second husband exclaimed. "I would have thought you would bring her flowers."

The first husband shrugged. "What am I going to do with flowers."

"If you really think about it," a husband said, "sex never takes as long as it appears to take."

"Then whatever you do," his wife replied, "don't think about it."

"Have you been able to locate the G spot?" a young man who had become sexually active was asked.

"Not yet," he replied. "I haven't even begun looking for the A to F spots."

"My wife thinks sex is funny. She didn't smile all the time she was cleaning the house, or doing the laundry, or making dinner, or washing the dishes, or getting the kids ready for bed, but when I woke her up and suggested we make love, she couldn't stop laughing."

Sometimes there's justice.

"I have some good news and some bad news," a mistress said to her boyfriend.

"What's the good news?" he asked.

"I'll be able to make it tonight," she said.

"And what's the bad news?" he asked.

"Your wife is coming with me."

A father informed his children that it was time for them to have a talk about the birds and the bees.

"I think it would be a lot more interesting if you told us about the birds and the rabbits," one of the children responded.

It's more difficult to threaten older men when they miss an important occasion.

"You can forget all about sex until our next anniversary," one was informed after missing the occasion by a day.

"Only three hundred and sixty-four days," he replied. "That's not so long."

Wives are looking at their husbands across the room. Finally one of them remarks, "It's our own fault, we married them."

When men are together, they talk about women.

When women are together, they talk about men.

The only difference we've noticed so far is that women share a lot more laughter.

A middle-aged husband and wife were enjoying sex when they heard a sound.

"I know the kids have grown up and moved away," the wife said, "but for some reason I keep expecting them to knock on the bedroom door."

"I know," the husband replied. "So do I, but they won't, so quit worrying about it."

They resumed their love making until they heard another sound.

"Mom, Dad, anybody home?"

It's not that men don't make an effort to satisfy a woman's sexual needs. It's just that a person can only accomplish so much in three minutes.

A man who was supposed to pick up some condoms at the drug store, purchased a package of surgical gloves by mistake.

"Oh no," his girlfriend exclaimed. "No orgies."

Why is it? If a woman wears a bikini to wash the car in the driveway, she's nicely attired. If a man wears his pajamas to the driveway to get the newspaper, he's half naked.

"I had sex with your wife when you were out last night."

"So that's why she was laughing so hard when I got home."

On their wedding night, a husband suggested to his bride, "Let's make love."

"I knew it," she replied. "You're just like all my other husbands."

A husband forgot an anniversary.

His wife informed him, "That's not the only thing you can forget about."

"I decided to surprise my wife last night when she came home from her two week business trip," one husband said to another, "so I asked our doctor to prescribe a medication to increase our sexual pleasure."

"Did the medication work?" the other husband asked.

"I'll say," said the first husband. "It gave me an erection that lasted all evening."

"How did you wife feel about it?"

"I don't know. She missed her flight."

"What was the most interesting place you ever made love?" a college student was asked.

"A taxi," he replied.

"I'll bet the taxi driver was upset."

"No. He didn't even know we were on his taxi."

A leading man in romantic movies was asked, "Do you prefer making love to taller women, shorter women, heavier women, lighter women, red heads, brunettes, blondes, women with light complexions, dark complexions . . . ?"

"Yes," he answered.

A father was talking to his teenage son.

"Are you angry because I came in so late last night?" the son asked.

"No, it's not that," his father replied. "I just wanted to find out how you did it without waking your mother."

First wife: "My husband and I made love right up until the very end."

Second wife: "Oh, I'm sorry. His death . . . ?"

First wife: "No, silly, the divorce."

The differences between sex when you're twenty and sex when you're sixty:

At twenty, it's two minutes of talk, an hour of foreplay, and two hours of sex.

At sixty, it's two hours of talk, which is considered foreplay, and two minutes of sex, if you're up to it.

"Last night I informed my girlfriend that I was breaking up with her. She said that she would like to perform an exotic striptease for me that she was sure would change my mind."

"Did you change your mind?"

"Did I!!! By the time she was finished, I was so sexually excited I never wanted to leave her."

"And what did she do?"

"She put on her clothes and went home."

"Do you want real or imaginary sex tonight?" a wife said.

"What's the difference?" her husband asked.

"Real sex includes real flowers and real romance and real foreplay," she answered.

"And imaginary sex . . . ?"

"An imaginary barbed wire fence down the middle of the bed."

"Yes! Yes! Yes!!!!": Sometimes whispered by a woman during sex, sometimes when the sex is over.

Coming: A pathetic tone a wife uses when her husband has finally talked her into going to the bedroom.

Innocent bride on wedding night: "Do other people know about this?"

Those who can have sex, have sex. Those who can't have sex, talk about sex: There seems to be an awful lot of talk about sex.

Sexual favors: Alcohol, jewelry, dinners . . . .

Anti-climax: What your aunt has when your uncle does it right.

No frills sex: What women sometimes provide men with. No frills, no sex.

A husband asked his wife if they could make love. She said, "I have a headache."

So he gave her an aspirin. She said, "I still have the other headache."

He said, "What other headache?"

She said, "The one I had last night when I thought you were going to ask me."

"I once had an affair with an older man," one young woman said to another, "but he had a heart attack."

"Was it the sex?" the other young woman asked.

"I'm not sure if it was the sex," she replied, "or his wife breaking down the door."

"Do you and your husband ever make love when sports is on television?" one wife asked another.

"Occasionally, during half time," the second wife replied.

"That should give you quite a few enjoyable minutes," the first wife said.

"Did I mention that he also has time to make a sandwich, gather some snacks, go to the bathroom, and get another beer from the refrigerator."

"My wife just thanked me for the extremely expensive pearl necklace and earrings I bought her for our anniversary," a husband said.

"How much did they cost?" he was asked.

"Search me," he replied. "I'm still trying to figure out when our anniversary was."

"My husband and I like to babysit our neighbors' children every once in a while," one newlywed wife said to another.

"Does it encourage you to want children?" the other newlywed wife asked.

"No," the first newlywed wife replied. "It encourages us to practice birth control."

"Five thousand years ago, an abundance of sex was believed to provide man with eternal happiness."

"How would anyone prove that?"

"They dug up a five thousand year old man who believed in it."

"That wouldn't prove that an abundance of sex brought eternal happiness."

"Yes it would."

"How?"

"He was still smiling."

Men were talking.

"The first time my girlfriend and I made love," one of them said, "she asked me how many hours I thought it would take. I was laughing so hard, I almost forgot what I was doing."

A woman walked into a bar.

"I'm looking for a husband," she said.

"What about that guy over there?" the bartender suggested. "He's available."

"I'm not looking for a new husband," she replied. "I'm looking for the old one. He didn't come home last night."

"My husband and I approach making love in the same way we would read a good book," a wife said.

"What kind of book do you enjoy?" she was asked.

"Eight hundred pages of passionate romance."

"What kind of book does your husband enjoy?"

"Two hundred pages of hot steamy sex."

"Which book do you normally get?"

"That's the interesting part. We never know until we start reading."

Wife to husband crawling into bed at two o'clock in the morning: "Is that you?"
Husband: "Yes . . . . Who else might you have been expecting . . . ?"

"Does your wife like to tell you what she wants in bed?"
"I'll say. Even when I'm out in the kitchen preparing dinner, I can still hear her yelling."

"Are you upset because your husband is always bothering you to have sex?" one woman asked another.
"No," the other woman replied. "I'm upset because he isn't bothering me to have sex."

Golfers . . . .
A male golfer thinks he can hit the ball farther with a shorter club than he really can. A female golfer will choose a longer club, and still be disappointed with the results. A true golfer, on the other hand, can play the game with an old putter and a pile of enthusiasm, and enjoy every minute of it. I can't get over it, the more I think about golf the more it reminds me of sex.

A woman was complaining to a friend.

"I'll never go out with another man," she said. "Everyone told me what a nice person he was, then he took advantage of me, cheated on me, and left me for another woman."

"That's because you didn't know anything about him when you met," the friend said. "Let me introduce you to a co-worker of mine."

"Do you know what he's like?"

"Yes. He's such a nice person . . . ."

Young woman to mother on wedding day:

"When we were going together, he kept saying he couldn't wait to have sex. Now he says he can't wait to consummate the marriage. What's going to be next?"

First husband: "Does your wife like to engage in intimate conversation?"
Second husband: "Yes. She'll do anything to avoid having sex."

First woman: "Have you ever thought about trying online sex?"
Second woman: "No. I still prefer men."

"My husband's a little angry with me."

"Why?"

"He said he thought he might be losing some of his skills as a lover."

"But why would he be angry with you?"

"Because I might have said, don't worry about it, you don't have that many to lose."

First woman: "Have you ever allowed your body to become totally uninhibited?"

Second woman: "Yes I have. Oh, I thought you said uninhabited."

A client was negotiating with the madam in a house of prostitution.

"How much do you charge?" he asked.

"$500 per hour," she replied.

The client thought about it for a moment and then asked, "How much for two minutes?"

I said to my wife, "Do you feel like sex?"

She replied, "You'll get a lot more with sugar than you'll get with vinegar."

Just when I was getting used to bringing her flowers . . . .

"Does your husband talk to you during sex?" one wife asked another.

"Not usually," the other wife answered. "It's difficult for him to talk and puff at the same time."

First man: "How do you feel about legalized prostitution?"
Second man: "No thanks. I've decided to stay single."

"I think they should legalize prostitution and let the government look after it," one man said to another.

"That would be one way to drive them out of business," the other man answered.

"I came home a little inebriated last night," a husband said. "There were three women in my bed. One was a movie star, one was a stripper, and one was my wife. I couldn't decide which one I should make love to."

"Which one did you finally choose?" he was asked.

"It didn't make any difference," he said. "No matter which one I chose, I got my wife."

One prostitute told another she was taking up golf because she heard she could find a lot of good lays there.

The other prostitute replied, "That's lies, you idiot."

"Are you and your husband having any luck conceiving?" one wife asked another.

"Yes," the other wife replied.

"You mean you have?" the first wife asked.

"No, I mean we haven't," the second wife replied.

An older man and a younger man meet on the way to work.

Older man: "What did you do last night?"

Younger man: "My girlfriend and I just frittered away the evening."

Older man: "Is that what they're calling it now."

The secret to a satisfying and fulfilling sexual relationship between a husband and wife is the unselfish sacrifice each of them puts forth to make sure the other is happy . . . or so each of them keeps saying . . . .

"I was once asked, if I had to choose between watching sports on T.V. every weekend for the rest of my life, or having the opportunity to enjoy sex even one time during the rest of my life, which would I choose."

"That was a strange question. Who asked it?"

"My wife."

"My husband sometimes becomes amorous in his sleep."

"Oh? Does it affect your love making?"

"One of our pillows seems to be enjoying it."

Wife: "Who goes there?"
Husband: "That's what I get for marrying a woman who used to be in the army."

"Men are after just one thing," a mother informed her daughter, "and you must never let them have it until after you're married."

On their next date, the daughter informed her boyfriend, "I'm really sorry, but Mom says you can't drive Dad's Cadillac until after we're married. We'll have to have sex in your car again."

Women tend to look at love emotionally, while men tend to approach it from a physical aspect.

For instance, a woman might say, "My heart is longing for you," while a man could mean another part of the body entirely.

Husband: "I'm just as good at making love as my friend, Ralph."
Wife: "I'm interested in knowing just how you discovered this."

"Have you had good luck in marriage?" a woman was asked.
"Yes," she replied, "all six of them."

Men were discussing opening lines they used when meeting a woman.

"I used to open with, would you make love to me for a diamond necklace," one of them replied, "and every once in a while I got lucky, but then I met a woman who said she was in the jewelry business and she knew it wasn't real."

"What line do you open with now?"another man asked.

"What business are you in?"

"In answer to the question, would prolonging the sex act bring more happiness to your wife, I ask you, would three minutes bring her any more pleasure than two minutes?"

Man in bar: "How about having sex with me?"
Woman in bar: "Go screw yourself."
Man in bar: "If I could do that, I wouldn't be bothering you, would I."

A man and woman both lied. She promised that after they were married she would give him sex any time he liked, and he promised he would give her romance and unending passion.

A health insurance plan said they would pay for pills that would improve a husband's sexual reception. He wanted to know if they would also work on the sports channel.

Asked to explain the difference between being a virgin and being a non virgin, one woman said to another. "I've found it a lot easier remaining a non virgin."

"We had a power failure in our area last night," a husband said, "and I thought it would be a good time to fool around with the wife. It took three hours."

"To have sex ????"

"To find her."

A grandmother was asked how many different ways she had made love.

She answered, "There's more than one?"

A man and woman met in a bar. She agreed to go home with him to make love.

On the way, she asked, "Do you have a condom?"

"No," he replied, "just an apartment."

A single man was complaining to a married man about how much it cost him to have sex.

"First you have to buy her flowers," he said, "then there's dinner and drinks, then there's a movie or a play, then if you're lucky . . . ."

The married man laughed and said, "Wait until you get married and see how much it costs you. First she goes shopping . . . ."

"How do you get your husband's attention when he's watching football?" one wife asked another.

"I once stood in front of the T.V., naked," the second wife said.

"Did he notice you?" the first wife asked.

"No," the second wife replied. "But the other husbands did."

"Did you get any reaction from the other husbands when you stood in front of them naked?" the first wife asked.

"I certainly did," she replied.

"What did they say?"

"Down in front."

"Have you tried being naked at other times?" she was asked.

"Yes," she replied. "Once when my husband was watching football on the T.V. in the living room, I took off all my clothes in the kitchen, stood on the table, and told him what I was doing."

"What did he say?"

"While you're out there, bring me another beer."

Husbands were bragging about their sex drives. All except one.

"My wife and I don't seem to be enjoying sex as often as we used to," he said.

"What appears to be the problem?" he was asked.

"I'm not quite sure," he said. "Yesterday it was O.K. Last night it was O.K. This morning it was O.K. This afternoon it was O.K. But this evening . . . ."

Slightly inebriated man to slightly inebriated woman in bar: "Of course I'll marry you if you let me make love to you. What was your name again?"

"What a week I've had," one husband said to another. "First of all, my wife stopped giving me sex because she said I enjoyed playing golf more than I enjoyed making love to her . . . and then I couldn't get a tee time for Thursday, Friday, and Saturday."

"Is it normal to find humor in sex?"
"Yes. Especially when we're not getting any."

Doctor: "Your wife appears to be having some difficulty getting pregnant, and we're considering trying something different. How do you feel about ejaculating into a test tube?"
Husband: "What kind of test tube?"

Women!!!!

Before we get married, they say to us, "I'll make love to you anytime you need it."

After we're married, they say to us, "You don't need that right now."

"Has your husband ever provided you with unending ecstasy?" one woman asked another.

"Yes," the other woman answered. "Once."

"How long did it last?"

"He left three years ago last month."

Men were discussing how they might get their wives more interested in sex.

"Have you given any thought to trying flowers?" asked one.

"I suppose," the other answered, "but I don't see how they would be any better than what I'm using now."

Slightly inebriated man in bar: "What would it take to get you into bed?"
Woman in bar: "With you? Probably double pneumonia."
Slightly inebriated man in bar: "So, how do you feel . . . ?"

A wife came up with a sexual variation that sometimes kept her husband going for two or three days. When they were finished, she said, "That should keep you going for two or three days."

An American girl's boyfriend immigrated to Italy and became an Italian citizen. She was ecstatic.

"Why so happy?" she was asked.

"Because I've heard Italians are so amorous," she replied.

"Did you marry your husband for his wealth, or for his skills as a lover?" a young wife was asked.

"Neither," she replied, "but I wouldn't mind if he came up with one or the other."

A husband who felt a little deprived suggested to his wife, "I think we should run our sexual lives in the same way we run our corporation. On the quota system."

His wife replied, "Don't worry, you're making your quota."

Female intuition: Allows a woman to develop a headache before a man even asks.

"What would it take for you to make love to me?" a man said to a woman.

"It would take at least three bottles of wine," she responded.

"You can drink three bottles of wine . . . ?" he exclaimed.

"No," she replied. "I can only drink one glass. But it would take three bottles."

"Last weekend a friend of mine married a woman who said she would make love to him every second, of every minute, of every day, until death do them part," one man told another.

"How did he make out?"

"I don't know. He died yesterday."

One town was so small they couldn't afford a house of prostitution. They had a 1983 Buick of prostitution.

You know you're in a small town when you ask the clerk at an ice cream store where the local hot spot is, and he replies, "This is it."

Whatever was God thinking when he came up with the system we use for making children?

A husband was looking for ways to increase their savings.

"How about each time we make love, I give you some money," he said to his wife.

"How much money did you have in mind?" she asked.

"How about ten dollars?"

"You spent more than that *before* we were married."

Woman: "I wouldn't be caught dead in bed with you."
Man: "If you die, I'll stop."

"Would you say that there are many faults in your marriage?" one wife asked another.

"Just one little one," the second wife replied. "Here he comes up the driveway now."

As usual, wives were sharing laughter at the expense of their husbands.

"I was in the mood for sex last night," one said, "but my husband wasn't."

"What excuse did he give?" another asked.

"He said he had to get up in the morning," the first wife replied.

"Men," the other wife scoffed. "Like losing two minutes sleep is going to make a difference."

A husband goes to a doctor. He has a problem with his penis.

The doctor says, "You don't need me. I'm a proctologist."

The husband says, "You're exactly what I need. I asked my wife for sex last night. She was a little angry with me and told me, no."

"So, why do you need a proctologist?" the doctor asks.

The husband answers, "I said to her, what do you expect me to do with this . . . ?"

"My mother told me to be patient, and the right man would eventually come along," one woman said to another.

"And did he?" the other woman asked.

"Not yet."

"You mean you have never married?"

"Yes, I've been married."

"How long did it last?"

"It will be twenty-seven years, next month."

A husband wanted to know what it would take to get his wife more interested in sex.

His wife suggested, "Dinner . . . an evening on the town. . . romance . . . foreplay . . . ."

"Well, make up your mind," he said. "I don't have time for them all."

Males don't realize it when they are young, but beating up boys is a girls way of showing affection. Later on they show their affection by letting us carry their fifty pound back pack home from school. Then they show their affection by letting us buy them dinners and movies and flowers and jewelry. The ultimate affection is when we die and leave them everything we own.

Two wives were doing a little comparing.

"The only problem my husband and I have," said one, "is coming up with enough variety to make our sex last an hour and a half. Do you ever have that problem?"

"Not so far," the second wife replied. "The only problem we have is deciding what we should do for the remaining hour and twenty-eight minutes."

Sex - men - stages:

First they wonder what it is. Then they wonder how they can get it. Then they wonder how they ever got along without it. Then they wonder what they can take to still do it. Then they wonder what all the fuss was about.

Sex - women - stages:

First they wonder what it is. Then they wonder what they should do about it. Then they wonder if they should give it away or hang on to it. Then they wonder how many times they should give it away or hang on to it. Then they wonder what they can prescribe for their husbands so they can still hang onto it. Then they also wonder what all the fuss was about.

"I asked my wife to give me one good reason why we couldn't have sex last night," one husband said to another.

"What did she say?" asked the other husband.

"She said she could not only give me one good reason, she could give me ten good reasons."

"What were they?"

"No, no, no, no, no, no, no, no, no, no."

A sexy young thing married an eighty year old man with promises that she would make love to him every night. After two months she changed her mind.

"Why?" he asked.

"To tell you the truth," she said, "I didn't think you would last this long."

An elderly man was flirting with a vivacious young woman.

"I'd like to go out with you," she said, "but I'm a little concerned that you won't be able to satisfy my sexual needs. What would you do if you had difficulty getting an erection?"

"I'd just invite a few of my friends over," he replied. "I figure that between the five of us, we should be able to come up with something."

One way to tell if we will make good husbands and wives is to look at the relationships between our older relatives . . . our fathers and mothers, our grandparents, our aunts and uncles . . . or maybe we could just take a look at ourselves.

"When do you know you have gone too far?" a college student was asked.

"When I find a girl who will go all the way," he replied, "and then I leave her for one who won't go all the way."

"I'm just not getting the satisfaction from love making that I think I should be getting," one woman said to another.

"Why don't you try what I do," the second woman answered. "When I make love, I think of going shopping or having some rich chocolate cake, and for some reason it lets me enjoy it more."

When they met again, the second woman asked, "Well, did you try thinking about going shopping or having some rich chocolate cake?"

"Yes," the first woman replied.

"And how did it make you feel?"

"Like going shopping and having some rich chocolate cake."

A woman was asked if she had ever taken a course in sexual relations.

"Yes, every time I date," she replied. "Of course I'll still love you in the morning, of course I care about your feelings, of course I'm only thinking about your pleasure, of course I'll never forget you, of course I want to marry you . . . ."

The difference between younger men having sex and older men having sex:

Younger men don't know what they're doing.

Older men don't know what they're doing either, but older women aren't quite so fussy.

"I discovered something new today," one husband said to another. "I discovered that the scent of flowers in the air heightens a woman's desire to make love."

"Did you read that in a book?" the other husband asked.

"No," the first husband replied. "My wife told me."

First woman: "Have you lost your virginity?"
Second woman: "Just the one time."

A wife purchased creams that were supposed to increase her bust size. After the first treatment, she said to her husband, "Would you like to borrow some?"

Two New Yorkers were talking.

"My girlfriend is playing hard to get," said one.

"How can you tell?" asked the other.

"She stopped giving me sex," said the first.

"When?"

"When she got married and moved to California."

"My girlfriend treats me like a dog," one man complained to another.

"In what way?" the other man asked.

"Every time I touch her leg, she says, down boy."

A couple decided they might be ordering take-out food a little too often when the husband asked, "Can we have sex tonight?" and his wife replied, "Sure, why not, what's their phone number?"

You might suspect your wife is just a wee bit angry with you when she says . . .

- "I would tell you why not, if I were speaking to you . . . ."

- "I'm sorry, I have a headache, and I intend to have one for quite a while . . . ."

- "If I were you, sweety, I'd be getting extra blankets, because I feel a chill a comin' . . . ."

- "You'll be going it alone tonight, stranger. . . ."

- "I hope you have a good imagination, because you're going to need it for a few days . . . ."

- "No, I can't recall the last time we made love, and I can't recall the next time either . . . ."

- "Of course I forgive you. Now leave me alone."

"If you discovered you had only two months to live," a husband was asked, "how would you spend it?"

"I'd spend it making love," he answered.

His wife interrupted, "Did he say two months, or two minutes . . . ?"

"How is your sexual relationship?" a marriage counselor asked a husband and wife.

"Fine," said the husband.

"Not very romantic," said the wife.

"What about trying something different to help your relationship," the counselor suggested, "like a vacation to some exotic faraway land."

The husband and wife agreed to give it a try. A month later they were back in session.

"How was your vacation?" the counselor asked.

"Wonderful," the wife replied. "I never felt so romantic."

"And you?" he asked the husband.

"About the same," he replied.

"Didn't your vacation to the exotic, faraway land make you feel more romantic?" the counselor asked.

"Why would I go?" the husband replied. "I'm not the one having a problem with romance."

Why is it, women give sex and men get sex?

"Is your husband very romantic?"

"Sometimes yes, sometimes no."

"Do you let him know when you think he's romantic?"

"Yes."

"What do you tell him when he's not romantic?"

"I still tell him he's romantic."

"Why?"

"For some reason, it makes him more romantic."

"I would have had great sex last night, except for my wife," a husband said.

"Why?" he was asked. "What did she do?"

"She woke up."

"I finally found a way to get my wife more excited during our love making," one husband said to another.

"How?" the other husband asked.

"Half way through, I mentioned that there was a sale ad in this morning's newspaper."

Men soon discover there is a difference between having sex and making love.

They pay a few dollars for sex.

They pay in other ways for making love. Many, many, many, many other ways.

"I think that part of our love making could be getting a little rusty," a husband said.

"Maybe it's because you're not using that part often enough," his wife replied.

"I'm going over to my girlfriend's place tonight, hopefully for sex," a boyfriend said.

"Only sex?" he was asked.

"Yes."

"What about foreplay?"

"No. No play. Just sex."

"It costs a lot of money to have sex in Las Vegas," one husband said to another.

"How would you know something like that?" the other husband asked.

"When my wife lost all her money," the first husband replied, "and then she lost all my money, we had nothing else to do, so we had sex."

"I think I'm going to have to be more explicit when I suggest to my husband that I might enjoy dinner for two, flowers, and romance before we make love. Last night he brought home two hamburgers, a yellow weed he found growing in the sidewalk, and a book of erotica."

"Every night, my husband asks me for the same thing."

"Is he continually wanting sex?"

"No. He's continually losing the remote control for the T.V."

A little boy was asked if he knew the date he was conceived.

"I'm not sure," he replied. "My Mom and Dad say I was there . . . but darned if I can remember."

Fortune teller: "I see you losing something. Something to do with your virginity."

Woman: "I lost my virginity seven years ago to my husband."

Fortune teller: "Hmmm . . . ? Have you seen your husband lately . . . ?"

"Aren't you aware that too many drinks will cause you to give in to temptation?" one woman informed another.

"I'm not only aware of it," the other woman replied. "I'm counting on it."

"Have you ever made love in a car?" a college student was asked.

"Once," she replied.

"How was it?" she was asked.

"Not bad," she replied, "but it didn't last as long as I would have liked."

"How come?"

"The light changed."

Before making love, a woman enjoys flowers, a romantic dinner for two, intimate conversation, cuddling, foreplay . . . . A man enjoys a bra with an easy release fastener.

A husband's idea of a sensible gift for his wife is sheer lingerie.

A wife's idea of a sensible gift is sheer lingerie with a receipt, so she can exchange it for a flannel nightgown.

A man approached an attractive woman in a bar.

"I dreamed I made love to you last night," he said.

"Oh?" she replied. "How did it turn out?"

"It was the most fantastic sex I ever had," he exclaimed.

She shrugged. "Then what do you need me for?"

Anybody that says sex is overrated, either isn't doing it right, or at all.

"I couldn't make love to my husband last night because I had a headache, chills, and a fever."

"Did you, really?"

"No, not really, but just telling him I had a headache didn't appear to be working."

A wife was talking to her husband again, but she wasn't quite ready to forgive him.

He said that in anticipation of making up after two days of not speaking, he had bought a book on how to enjoy love making.

She replied, "Oh, a do-it-yourself book."

"My wife says she's leaving me because I'm a lousy lover," one husband said to another.

"Don't be so hard on yourself," the other husband replied. "I'm sure she's leaving you for other reasons too."

"If you had three wishes, what would you wish for?" a wife was asked.

"I would wish for my husband to be the greatest lover in the world," she answered.

"Wait a minute," her husband interrupted. "Last night while we were making love, you said I was the greatest lover in the world."

"You should never believe anything I say when I'm in the middle of doing something," his wife replied.

"One part of me wants to make love, and one part of me doesn't," a wife said.

"Well, let me know which part does," her husband replied, "so I'll know where to begin."

What we don't know about sex could fill a book. Many authors have done just that, filled a book with everything they know nothing about.

Women have been known to marry their husbands for their holdings. Holding flowers, holding doors, holding hands, holding and hugging . . . .

Wives were discussing their sex lives.
First wife: "Last night I asked my husband if he knew how long it would take him to finish. He said to give him a couple of minutes."
Second wife: "How long had you been making love, up to that point?"
First wife: "We hadn't started yet."

First wife: "My husband asked me what I'd like for our anniversary. I said that all I wanted was half an hour of making love."
Second wife: "And did he give it to you?"
First wife: "Yes. Two minutes on Tuesday, two minutes on Thursday, two minutes on . . . ."

"I know an eighty-seven year old man who married a twenty-three year old woman. After three months, he couldn't take it anymore."
"Heart attack . . . ?"
"Wore out."

A man was trying to make time with a woman in a bar. After a while the conversation came around to sex.

"In your dreams," she said.

"I already did that," he replied. "It got the job done, but this way is a lot more fun."

"Shortly after we were married, I suggested to my wife that we become celibate."

"Did she agree to it?"

"Yes."

"But you have six children."

"I know. I asked her about it. She said she was looking into it."

A husband is getting his annual checkup. One of the questions the doctor asks is, "Are you and your wife enjoying an active sex life?"

"Unfortunately, I'm not able to perform sex right now," the husband replies.

So the doctor prescribes some pills to increase his libido. A month later he returns.

"How is sex with your wife now?" the doctor asks.

"Much better," the husband replies. "She came home yesterday."

"Last night I told my husband that he's the best lover in the world," one wife informed another.

"That's nice," the other wife replied, "but what would you tell him if he was the worst lover in the world?"

"What do you think I've been doing," the first wife replied.

"I used to enjoy wine, women, and song," a middle-aged man complained, "but not anymore. First I had to give up wine, then I had to give up women . . . and now my voice is going."

"What I'd like to know," a young student said to the teacher in her health education class, "is what does studying all these birds and bees and flowers have to do with my mother and father having sex and pollinating, anyway . . . ?"

A husband was watching an adult movie.

"And just how is this going to help our sex life?" his wife asked.

Her husband thought for a moment. "Visual aids . . . ?"

"My husband made love to me for more than two hours last night," one wife informed another. "The poor man was exhausted. But it was the most fulfilling evening of our marriage. I would have been happy with only half that time."

"Your husband will be happy to hear that," the other wife said.

"No he won't," the first wife replied.

"Why not?"

"I'm not going to tell him."

Asked why it took him only two minutes to make love, a man replied, "The last time I made love, it took me three minutes, and the woman began looking at her watch. I don't want to go through that embarrassment again."

"I wasn't enjoying sex as much as I thought I should," one woman said to another, "so my doctor prescribed some tranquilizers to help me relax."

"And are you enjoying having sex now?" the other woman asked.

"No," the first woman replied, "but for some strange reason I've been enjoying *not* having sex, more."

I miss the old days . . . .

In the old days a woman talked to her husband about having children. Now she talks to a laboratory.

A fifty year old man and a twenty-five year old man were discussing sex.

"There sure are a lot of different ways to make love now," the older man said.

"I know what you mean," the younger man replied. "I'd like to go back to the good old days, when there were just a hundred or so."

"I feel really bad about cheating on my wife," an unfaithful husband moaned.

"How bad?" another man asked.

"Two black eyes, three broken teeth, and some bruises from going down the stairs."

"My wife and I made love," one husband said to another. "Then I suggested we make love again. But she said I needed some time to rest up and cool down. It's been two weeks. You'd think I'd be rested up and cooled down by now."

A newlywed wife was complaining after a week of honeymooning.

"Nothing but sex, sex, sex," she said. "We had sex in the morning, sex in the afternoon, sex in the evening . . . ."

"Every day?" a friend asked.

"Not every day," the bride replied. "Monday we had sex in the morning, Thursday we had sex in the afternoon, Sunday we had sex in the evening . . . ."

A husband asks his wife for sex. Twenty-five years later he makes another request.

"What!" she exclaims. "Again!!??"

When did Adam learn that he was no longer the stronger sex?

Shortly after God said, "Adam, it's only a rib. What can I do with a rib?"

A couple were getting over a disagreement.

He said, "I apologize."

She said, "Forget about it."

He said, "Do you want to fool around?"

She said, "Forget about it."

There's no use reminding a man that he completed the sex act in two minutes. Most men would consider that a compliment.

"My husband did something on our last anniversary that he's never done before," a wife informed some other wives.

"What was that?" she was asked.

"He remembered it," she replied.

"Do you like to whisper anything special in a woman's ear when you want to make love to her?" a man about town was asked.

"Yes," he said. "Another glass of wine . . . ?"

A wife wouldn't give her husband sex, so he went shopping for a car. He figured, one way or another, he was going to get screwed.

A husband and wife were really tired.

Wife: "I'm sorry I fell asleep while we were making love last night."

Husband: "That's all right, I think I might have dozed off a couple times myself."

Man: "I'm not just looking for sex, you know."
Woman: "Boy, did you just miss an opportunity."

"Do you and your husband enjoy a glass of wine when you're having sex?" a wife was asked.
"We used to, but we had to stop," she replied.
"Drinking too much wine?"
"Kept spilling it."

"The last time I had sex, it cost me a hundred and fifty dollars."
"That wouldn't happen if you had a wife."
"That was my wife."

"Have you tried any of the new ways of making love?" a wife was asked.
"No," she replied.
"Why not?" she was asked.
"The old way seems to get the job done."

Aging affects men and women differently. As men get older they don't require as much sex. As women get older they don't have as many headaches.

Wives were doing some comparing.

"My husband only lasted two minutes last night," said one wife.

"That's unbelievable," exclaimed the other wife. "I'm going to tell my husband."

"That my husband only lasted two minutes?" said the first wife.

"No," replied the second wife. "That a husband *can* last two minutes."

"The way to a man's heart is through his stomach."

"That may be true, but there's a better way to get to other parts of his body."

A wife was reading a book on sex called 'How To Get Your Lover To Give You A Two Hour Orgasm', when another wife dropped by.

"What I want to know," the other wife said, "is how does he manage to get all that done in three minutes."

"Am I a great lover?" a husband asked.

"You're every bit as good now as you were on our wedding night," his wife answered.

"**Would you be jealous if I told you that your wife was asked by that man over there if she would make love to him for a million dollars?**" a husband was asked.

"**That depends,**" he replied. "**Will she be home in time to make dinner?**"

"**Sex education is very similar to most other educations,**" one college student said to another, "**except more fun. Even when we don't learn anything, it's still more fun.**"

Husbands are always competing. One was watching television at lunchtime when a friend telephoned.

"**What have you been up to today?**" the friend asked.

"**Well,**" the husband answered. "**I woke up at seven o'clock this morning, and my wife asked me to make love to her . . . why are you interrupting us.**"

Sex to some people is just a filthy, disgusting, immoral, degrading act. Unless, of course, they are the ones that are doing it.

"I called my wife to let her know I'd be getting home a little late," a husband who was out with some other husbands said. "She told me that was all right. She even said we could try a new way of making love when I got home. Does anybody know what the abstinence position is?"

"How do you tell when your wife is no longer angry with you?" one husband asked another.

"When she stops referring to me as, *What's His Name*," the other husband replied.

"Don't forget that sex can be a lot of fun," an older married man advised a newlywed.

"Are you just discovering that now?" the newlywed asked.

"No," the older man replied. "I discovered it shortly after our wedding when my wife and I had our first fight, and she said to me, don't forget, sex can be a lot of fun."

A man was trying to make time with a woman.

"Go to hell," she said.

"Okay," he replied. "Are women friendlier there?"

"I like to wear my bifocal glasses to bed," a wife explained to some other wives. "Depending on how I tilt my head, I can make some parts of my husband appear smaller, or other parts appear bigger."

A man gives his girlfriend jewelry and flowers and romantic dinners. Finally, hoping she might say yes, he suggests they make love.

"O.K.," she answers, "but next time why don't you try the other way?"

"What other way?" he says.

"Just ask me," she replies.

"I finally found the ideal man," one woman said to another. "He was kind, considerate, handsome, and sophisticated. He brought me flowers, opened doors, and took me to wonderful restaurants. He made love to me for hours. So I married him."

"Where is he?" the other woman asked. "I'd like to meet him."

The first woman gestured across the room. "He's that unshaven man over there on the sofa, watching T.V., drinking beer, and scratching himself."

Men and women look at the world differently. To a man, fooling around is *having* sex. To a woman, fooling around is *instead* of sex.

"Did you find it difficult to part with your virginity?" one woman asked another.

"Difficult?" the other woman replied. "I found it almost impossible."

First tipsy man in bar: "I came very close to having sex with a woman I met tonight."
Second tipsy man in bar: "How close?"
First tipsy man in bar: "She went home with the guy sitting next to me."

"My girlfriend said there would be no sex if I didn't bring her flowers and take her out for dinner," a young man said to a married man. "It's costing me a lot of money, but it's worth it."

"My wife told me the same thing," the married man replied.

"And is it costing you a lot of money?" the young man asked.

"Can't say that it is," the married man answered. "Right now I'm saving a fortune."

Two astronauts made love in outer space.

Male astronaut: "I didn't notice a difference."

Female astronaut: "I enjoyed the weightlessness."

A little boy was asked if his father was home.

"He went to work," the little boy replied. "But Joe the handyman is coming over to do some chores for Mommy, and Joe will know what time Daddy will be home."

"What time does Joe usually get here?" he was asked.

"Usually right after Daddy goes to work."

Husbands and wives hear things differently.

A wife might say, "Honey, how would you like to start a family . . . ?"

The husband will already be heading for the bedroom. He doesn't hear, "Start a family. . . ." All he hears is, "How would you like to . . . ."

"Is your wife good in bed?" a newlywed husband was asked.

"Yes," he replied. "That's the problem."

"How could that be a problem?"

"I'd like for her to be bad once in a while."

An Interview With The World's Foremost Authority On Sex

You claim to be the world's foremost authority on sex . . . .

Yes.

Just what is it that makes you the world's foremost authority on sex?

I have been studying sex my entire life.

When did you first become interested in sex?

At a very young age. I can remember asking my father where I came from.

What did he say?

Cleveland.

Did he give you any other explanation?

Yes. He said I was born in a cabbage patch.

Did he explain how you got to the cabbage patch?

He said the stork brought me.

Did you ask him where the stork got you?

Yes.

What did he say to that?

Ask your mother.

Where did your mother say you came from?

She said I came from an egg in her tummy.

And did this give you a clearer understanding of where you came from?

Not exactly.

Not exactly . . . ?

For a while there I thought was hatched.

Now just a minute. It doesn't appear to me that you had a very clear understanding of sex when you were young.

That may be true. But it wasn't because I didn't try to learn. I was sure there had to be some kind of connection between boys and girls. I just wasn't sure what the connection was.

Did you enjoy girls?

Yes.

Was there anything you especially enjoyed about girls?

I enjoyed fighting with them.

How did this affect your life?

I got beat up a lot.

After you grew older, did you still have this urge to fight with girls?

No.

No . . . ?

No. But I had this other urge.

Did you know what this other urge meant?

No. But I asked some experts about it.

Could you tell me who these experts were? Were they doctors, sex therapists, psychologists, authors who had studied the subject . . . ?

No. The guys down at the pool hall.

The guys down at the pool hall . . . ????

Yes.

What did they say?

Man, are you dumb. Everybody knows about sex man. Man, if you don't know about sex, we're not going to tell you.

Did you ever find out why your friends wouldn't tell you about sex?

Sure. They didn't know any more than I knew.

Do you remember the first time you went out with a girl?

Yeah, I'll say. What a time that was.

What did you do?

We held hands.

What did you tell your friends you did?

I made up stories. I would tell them how romantic and exciting it was, but at the same time I would leave my description a little blurry and fuzzy, so that by the time I finished bragging, they didn't know whether I did or I didn't.

Didn't they ask questions?

No. They couldn't.

Why not?

Because I would just say, man are you dumb. Everybody knows about sex man. Man, if you don't know about sex, I'm not going to tell you.

Did you get all your education about sex from the guys down at the pool hall?

No. I spent a lot of time at the library, reading books.

Did you have any difficulty understanding these books?

A little. I didn't know what all the words meant.

What words?

Words like erogenous. That sounds like a margarine. Or vagina. I thought that was a city in Saskatchewan.

Up until now all your knowledge of sex appears to be theory. How did you go about getting practical experience?

I began chasing girls.

What were girls like when you were growing up?

I knew just two types of girls. Good girls and bad girls.

Did you ever go out with a bad girl?

No. But I met one once.

How did you know she was bad?

From the way she introduced herself.

What did she say?

Hi. My name is swinger. Want to go to bed?

What did you do?

I ran.

Did your friends down at the pool hall ever go out with bad girls?

One did. He went to a house of prostitution, but I don't think he was very good at it.

What makes you say that?

They gave him back change.

Did you ever go to a house of prostitution, yourself?

No, but I once joined a key club.

That must have been some experience. Did you have any luck?

Sure did. The first night I won a Mercedes.

Are you sure you know what a key club is?

All I know is, I went in with a Honda and came out with a Mercedes Benz. There was just one catch. The guy who owned it wouldn't give me the car unless I took his wife home.

When you took her home, did she invite you in?

Yes. She said, I guess it isn't every night a woman offers herself to you.

What did you say?

I said, are you kidding. It isn't every night I get to drive a Mercedes, and away I went.

You'll have to excuse me, but it seems to me that you've had an entire lifetime of bungling sex.

I suppose that's true. Fortunately a beautiful woman came into my life.

Who?

My wife.

I'm afraid to ask. Was she a good girl or a bad girl?

A good girl. Every time I wanted to be bad, she would quote her mother.

What did her mother say?

It takes a man to try ... and a woman to deny.

Did that bother you?

No. At least not until after we were married.

What happened then?

I said, you can stop saying that now.

Did your wife have any other defenses before you were married?

Yes.

What?

No.

No?

No. Actually, she used to say, no no no, *ten* thousand times no.

Did you ever break down her defenses?

A little. By the time we were married, she was only saying no no no, *nine* thousand times no.

What does she say now?

Is that all you married me for.

What types of excuses does she give you?

I'm too tired. You're too tired. You'll throw your back out. I have a headache. We'll wake the kids . . . .

You wouldn't want to wake the kids.

Our kids are twenty-five years old.

You're going to have to excuse me again, but I don't see how you could possibly be the world's foremost authority on sex. I've never seen anyone who has bungled sex as much as you have.

That's true. But they say you learn from your mistakes.

What have you learned?

I've learned that there is a lot more to sex than just sex.

Such as . . . ?

Love, caring, affection, enjoyment, devotion, understanding, intimacy, romance, conversation, friendship, sharing, giving. Yes, and sometimes just plain old passion and lusty desire.

Would you mind if we talk to your wife and ask her what it's like to be married to the world's foremost authority on sex?

If you don't mind, not right now.

Why not?

She says she has a headache.

* * * * * * * *

acadiascale.com

**Acadia Scale Press books
may be purchased at
amazon.com
barnes&noble.com
Barnes & Noble Book Stores
Borders Book Stores
borders.com
and other book and gift stores.**

**Most stores will be happy to order books
if they do not have a copy in stock.
Stores may order through
INGRAM BOOK COMPANY
and other book distributors.**